The Author wishes to express his gratitude to
Mons. BALDASSARE CALISTI, parish priest of the Cathedral of Monreale,
for his kind collaboration.

THE CATHEDRAL OF MONREALE

Monreale is the swan-song of the art of the Norman Age. Only a few passages survive today — but these are of unrivalled splendour — in the cathedral and the cloister at Monreale.

Monreale is, therefore, the culminating moment of an ideal "Itinerary of Norman Places of Artistic Interest" in Sicily, after the monuments of Cefalù and of Palermo; not the sole survivors of that age but the most significant ones.

Visitors, illustrious or otherwise, have arrived here and continue to do so with increasing fervour; each one of them responding as much as it is within him to respond. But no-one, once inside the cathedral, having viewed it from the Great Door can fail to respond to the singular experience that it offers: the majesty of its architecture, the clarity of it; and the splendour of its mosaics: intrinsically fused together like notes of music in perfect concord. For the immense tapestry of coloured glass tesserae — the most extensive array in Italy — does not alter the structures of the temple but only enriches them, it bathes them in a warm wave of gold and rainbow hues, it accompanies them and leads them forward to where the enormous bust of Christ with arms outspread as if to contain the universe, speaks, admonishes us that here all ends.

Memories will then come crowding in: here we find the grandeur of the Cathedral of Cefalù and the magnificence of the Palatine Chapel united in an architectonic — decorative organism that is new, or that is kindred to these latter monuments but possessing a beauty of its own that is quite unmistakable. A beauty that we shall savour by first observing the harmonious distribution of the whole and then turning our attention to the mosaics. Wherever our eyes take us — the first thing that arouses our curiosity, leaving aside any purely formal evaluation — the sentiments of men of almost a thousand years ago (but are they really such?) are revealed by a flicker of expression on a face, by a simple gesture. There lies revealed — a mere allusion transpiring from the inevitable fixedness and mineral congealment of mosaic — the two great sentiments of the two Testaments and of History: suffering and hope. And anger, unfortunately; and violence and betrayal, the great curses. But there is also serenity: more abstract that of the Saints and of the prophets, more deeply aware that imprinted on the face of Christ, who knows the price of it. Joy, on the contrary, is rare; as too, is happiness, except that conquered by asceticism: it will come, perhaps, at the end of time. But we are here, on Life's stage; here on earth as long as God should will it and we must remain here, content with the music of Mozart, with the rosy spires of the Dolomites, with a child's caress to its Mother's face. And with Monreale, an achievement that is an altar to Faith and to Beauty.

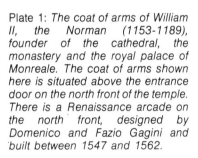

Plate 1: *The coat of arms of William II, the Norman (1153-1189), founder of the cathedral, the monastery and the royal palace of Monreale. The coat of arms shown here is situated above the entrance door on the north front of the temple. There is a Renaissance arcade on the north front, designed by Domenico and Fazio Gagini and built between 1547 and 1562.*

Plate 2: *The monumental group of buildings at Monreale seen from the air. Today it is the centre of this picturesque little town which lies at a short distance from Palermo on high ground offering a marvellous view of the Conca d'Oro. The best conserved buildings are the cathedral and the adjoining cloister on the south front. The Benedictine monastery and the royal palace which are now used for other purposes have undergone extensive alteration, particularly on the inside.*

Plate 3: *The west front of the cathedral on which stands the XVIII century Great Porch enclosed between two corner towers, typical of Norman architecture.*

Plate 4: *The stupendous, imposing absidal end of the cathedral, entirely covered with an intricate play of arches, miniature columns and rosettes, enriched by inlaid limestone and lavic stone.*

HISTORICAL BACKGROUND

We owe the foundation of the Cathedral of Monreale to William II, the last of the great Norman Kings of Sicily (1153 - 1189). Tradition has seen fit to designate this king as "the Good", in contrast with his predecessor William I, known as "the Bad". A tradition which was begun perhaps by Arab chroniclers of the period who describe the king in question — an athletic man with red hair — as being endowed with every human virtue, despite his taste for magnificence and a weakness for astrology. He was certainly no idler however (as some historians would have it) and his policy of centralizing monarchic power demonstrates this. Such a policy was inborn to the Normans, splendidly codified by Roger II and harshly applied by William I (he too, however, a lover of pomp and luxury) whose epithet was perhaps bestowed on him by his rebellious vassals. William II was no laggard in foreign policy either: he carried forward, in fact, the adventurous expansionism of the Normans of Hauteville, begun by the conquest of Southern Italy and of Sicily. He restrained the excesses of the Marine Republics of Genoa and Venice with well-planned treaties; he fought the Muslims in defence of the Holy Places and he too, set himself against the Eastern Empire, moving down on Byzantium: hankering perhaps to crown the dream of his forbears — to be seated on the illustrious throne of Constantinople. The principal feature of the reign of William II was — and this too is of distinctly Norman and later, Swabian stamp — to show the greatest bounty towards all the ethnic and religious components of the peoples conquered by him. This of course, as long as they were obedient to the sovereign "by Divine Right".

Good William II therefore, but also, and why not indeed, partaker of the good things in life, ambitious even in his works, so-called, of peace — destined to last for centuries. Nor could he be otherwise, having behind him those examples of magnificence, his grandfather Roger II, great founder of palaces and churches and his own father William I who also built, but above all brought to a conclusion the works begun by Roger II. Therefore, the construction of the monumental group of buildings at Monreale, together with the foundation of the Cathedral of Palermo, can be reliably interpreted as the fruit of an anxiety to prove worthy of a glorious dynastic tradition and, where possible, to outshine it.

With this premiss, it would seem only proper to relate, in the manner of pious legend, how the Cathedral of Monreale came into

3

being. The King then, while hunting in his park, was overcome by fatigue and fell asleep. A lady (the Madonna) appeared to him in a dream and indicated tho him the place where his father's treasure was hidden. Having unearthed it, William II decided, in gratitude, to erect a temple to the Virgin.

Where and when did the Cathedral of Monreale arise, conceived from its very beginning as a unit comprising both monastery and royal palace? On the slopes of Monte Caputo, on land that bore the name of Monte Reale because it had already, long before, perhaps since the times of the Arab Emirates, been Crown land. It was a hunting reserve with scattered hamlets and shepherd huts, animated by fallow-deer, roe-bucks, boars, and enclosed by walls with towers and a castle. There are those, like Domenico Benedetto Gravina ("il Duomo di Monreale" Palermo 1859) who suggest that the church and monastery were erected on pre-existent foundations. Even today the matter is *sub judice*.

The year when work began on the church, dedicated to the Madonna Assunta, was perhaps 1172 when William II ceased to be under the legal jurisdiction of his mother, Margaret of Navarre. By 1174 both the monastery and the royal palace were under way. By 1176 all the buildings must have reached an advanced stage of construction because William II granted a number of privileges — to be ratified later the same year by Pope Alexander III — to the monks of the convent. These monks were Benedictine Cluniae from the then flourishing and powerful Abbey of the Trinity at Cava dei Tirreni (*Congregazione Cavense*). A conclusive testimony to the extraordinary rapidity of the work — taking into consideration the colossal building site with all its workshops, the condition of the roads and the technical knowledge of the times — is the Papal bull of Lucius III dated

Plates 5 and 6: *The Great Door of the cathedral.*
An elegant bas-relief decoration in marble alternating with mosaic strips (see detail Pl. 6) frames the portal on the cathedral west front. This ornamentation was carried out, according to Salvini and Krönig, by some of the master craftsmen who worked on the cloister. But it is the bronze door that lifts the portal into the realm of Art. The author was Bonanno Pisano who signed and dated it in 1186. The leafs were cast in Pisa and brought by sea to Sicily where they had to be shortened on the site prior to hanging. They are made up of 42 panels, each of which illustrates a story inspired by the Sacred Scriptures, from the Creation of Adam *to the* Christ Enthroned blessing the world. The style is direct and essential and not infrequently touched with poetry. The explanatory texts are in highly abbreviated Latin that in one case (Caim uccise frate suo Abel) — *Cain kills his brother Abel* — gives way to the growing Italian language.

Plate 7: *The Great Door of the cathedral.*
Two panels by Bonanno Pisano: below, the Original Sin; *above,* Cain and Abel with their flocks at pasture prior to Cain's crime.

Plates 8 and 9: *The cathedral minor portal: two details.*
The bronze leafs of the minor portal are made up of 28 panels sculpted and signed by Barisano da Trani and installed here between 1186 and 1190. There are few sacred stories (the Crucifixion, *the* Resurrection, Christ blessing, *and the* Madonna Enthroned) *and these are set amongst mythological and profane images. In the work of Barisano the narrative commitment of Bonanno Pisano is replaced by a decorative intent inherited from Byzantine tradition.*

10

12

11

12

Plates 10 to 12: *The cathedral interior.*
A masterpiece of late Romanesque architecture, the interior of the cathedral consists of three aisles terminating in a transept and three apses. Latin elements (aisles), Byzantine (square plan transept crossing) and Arab elements (pointed arch arcading, ceiling and decorative motifs) concur to create a single organism of extraordinary harmony. An immense mosaic tapestry covers the greater part of the walls and the structural elements of the temple.

1183, in which praise is bestowed on the diligence of the building masters and the church is nominated Metropolitan — becoming Mother Church of an ecclesiatical province: the abbot of the monastery therefore assuming, *ispo facto*, the title of Archbishop. The bronze leafs by Bonanno Pisano for the Great Door of the church probably arrived in 1186 aboard Pisan ships; perhaps in the same year or the following one, the leafs by Barisano da Trani for the north front entrance reached their destination.

At the death of William II (1189), however, Monreale had not yet taken on definitive shape: Gravina tells us that the church was still without its paved floors, the marble facing of the lower extremities of the walls and the height of the north-west tower was little more than that of the roof of the church. Nothing was to change until the sixteenth century when the belfry crowned with merlons was added.

In view of the total absence of dates and names regarding the mosaics, comment on them will be postponed to later pages.

The original architectural lay-out of the monastery — noticeably that of the cloister — and of the royal palace, must have been established, at least according to the more widely accepted theories of today, in the period corresponding, approximately, to the death of William II. In the tumultuous period that followed on the death of William II, a period covering the short-lived reigns of Tancredi and of William III as well as the conquest by Henry VI of Swabia, known as the Cruel (1194), the abbey was despoiled of its riches and privileges and these cost no

little struggle to regain. However, ratification by Henry VI, Innocent III and Frederick II testify to the renewed benevolence of emperors and popes towards Monreale. It was, though, only after a century from the commencement of work (1267) that the church was solemnly consecrated by Rudolph, Bishop of Albano, envoy of Clement IV. It was dedicated to the Nativity of the Virgin, but also came to be called St. Maria la Nuova, probably to distinguish it from the church of the Martorana — St. Mary of the Admiral — that had been built in Palermo during the reign of Roger II. In the meantime, first the parents of William II, then the king himself and his brothers Roger and Henry were buried in the church. In the course of the early years of the Angevin reign in Sicily Charles d'Anjou ordered the burial in the church of some relics (heart and praecordia) of St. Louis IX, King of France, who had died of the plague at Tunis during the eighth crusade (1270) and had been immediately boiled to prevent contagion: these are the only relics of the Saint left to us after the pillage of the basilica of Saint-Denis during the French Revolution. The subsequent history of the temple is a story of repair-work, restoration, additions, re-arrangement and replacement, all of which has not however substantially altered its original appearance.

The fate of the monastery and the royal palace is quite a different story.

In synthesis, it may be said that their structures, particularly on the inside, have undergone considerable alteration. Modification of the convent began during the XVI century when part of it was transformed into an archiepiscopal residence (in 1599 moreover, the recently transformed chapel of St. Placidus was created) subsequently to undergo numerous alterations. In 1589 the royal palace underwent

Plates 13 and 14: *The cathedral columns and capitals.*
The three aisles are delimited by 18 antique granite columns and one in cipolin marble. These are crowned with magnificent capitals on which rest mosaic covered pulvins. The capitals are partly adorned with figures and partly derived from classical schemes, chiefly Corinthian and composite.
The age of the capitals and where they came from is not known: they probably date from the beginning of the Roman Empire.

Plate 15: *Detail of the ceiling*
Although a great part was rebuilt after the fire in 1811, the ceiling faithfully follows the Arab taste for polychrome geometricized decoration

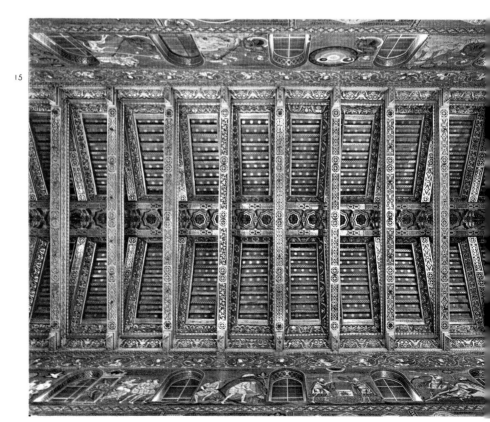

alterations and became a theological college, later to be reconstructed (1755). From 1795 to 1802 the Archbishop of Monreale ceased to benefit from an income; in 1866, in conclusion, the Benedictines left the convent. Today it is a State Art Institute for mosaic work. A masterpiece of Pietro Novelli da Monreale (at present under restoration) can still be seen there: a great canvas depicting *St. Benedict distributing the Rule, donating the symbolic bread to the religious and knights' orders* (1635). The most important repair work to the temple of Monreale chiefly involved the parts most subject to wear and tear such as the wooden ceiling (that remained for a century without any painted decoration) and the floors (covered in marble only in the second half of the sixteenth century). The choir and the organ were rebuilt on more than one occasion. Even the mosaics were cleaned, but they were restored and also altered. During the seventeenth century for example (the information is provided by Gravina) consideration was given to the idea of substituting some of the gold backgrounds under the

Plate 16: *The High Altar of the cathedral by Louis Valadier (1770-1773), a famous work of art in late baroque style with sculpture in silver and gold-plated bronze.*

Plate 17: *The altar-monument of St. Louis IX, King of France, containing relics of the Saint.*

Plate 18: The marble tombs of William I and William II (1575) situated in the right wing of the transept.

Plate 19: *The statue of St. John the Baptist (XVI century) placed in a niche decorated with a mosaic effigy of the Saint (south aisle).*

Plate 20: *The Chapel of St. Benedict. The Glory of St. Benedict, masterpiece of Ignazio Marabitti (1776).*

Plate 21: *The wooden statue of the venerated Madonna del Popolo (late XV century) on the baroque altar in the south-east, apse.*

Plate 22: *The Chapel of St. Benedict, an elegant late baroque setting, decorated with sculpture by G. B. Marino (1728).*

Plate 23: *The entrance to the Chapel of the Crucified Christ, an example of the late baroque style at its most luxuriant.*

feet of the protagonists with so many portions of earth, the argument being that the figures could not stand on air; the tesserae were subsequently washed down with wine. As with all ancient temples there have been moments of assiduous care and others of neglect: for example, in the late seventeenth century — this anecdote is also from Gravina — the church was infested with birds nests which were destroyed by setting birds of prey — pheasants imported from Spain — on them. Among the additions and the variations only the most significant follow: the first was the sacresty (end of the XV — beginning of the XVI century) followed by the north front arcade begun about 1547 by Gian Domenico and Fazio Gagini, of an ancient Lombard family of architects and sculptors, and concluded only in 1562. In 1561 the chapel of St. Benedict was installed in the more ancient one of St. Cataldo, only to be completely transformed in the eighteenth century. In 1575 the funerary monument in marble, of William II was sculpted. Then (1596) the chapel of St. Castrense, vastly modified in our century, was opened. Successively the chapel of the Crucified Christ (1686 - 1690) was completed — the most sumptuous Baroque architecture in the church; in these chapels were placed the funerary monuments of those of the archbishops who had shown most devotion to Monreale.

The greatest variants to the interior harmony of the temple were introduced by Archbishop Alfonso de los Cameros around 1660. Amongst others, the windows, originally of perforated lead plates, were replaced by glass, in this way illuminating the temple (and the mosaics) excessively and consequently provoking further intervention to attenuate the intensity of the light. Louis Valadier later created the precious High Altar of gold-plated silver.

26

There was no lack of misfortunes between the late eighteenth century and the early nineteenth. On Christmas Eve 1770 the portico on the west front (already reconstructed more than once) collapsed and was promptly substituted, on the orders of Cardinal Francesco Testa, by another one in Doric style designed by the canon Antonio Romano and built by the famous Ignazio Marabitti of Palermo. In 1807 a thunderbolt struck the south-west corner tower, cutting off the end of the spire.

The gravest of all was the fire of 1811 caused by the carelessness of an altar-boy. The ceiling, the organs, the choir were burnt, the columns supporting the funerary monuments of the two Williams collapsed, the other monuments were damaged. The consequent long period of rooflessness of the temple ended by damaging the cohesion of the mosaics that had to be re-attached by stages (note, in connection, the Bourbon coat of arms in the presbitory intrados, under the medallion containing a bust of Noah). The roof was under reconstruction from 1816 to 1824, its decoration was commenced and this continued until 1838. A list of all the works carried out since then would be a long one. Of these, brief mention must be made of the reconstruction of the choir-stalls, the replacement of the organ with a very modern one (1967) that, unfortunately, interrupts the view of the transept; the restoration of the royal tombs, the repairing of the fenestrations.

27

28

Plates 24 to 28: *The Chapel of the Crucified Christ and the Treasury.*
The Chapel of the Crucified Christ is a triumph of Sicilian baroque without rival in Italy for elaborate and imaginative decoration.
The chapel was designed by Fra. Giovanni da Monreale but carried out under the guidance of Angelo Italia di Licata (1686-1690). Adjacent to the chapel is the Treasury which contains precious antiques, among them a pastoral staff (pl. 24), and a monstrance (pl. 25); it is further enriched by a magnificent inlaid wooden cupboard, the work of Trapanese artists (pl. 28).

AESTHETIC APPRECIATION

Mention has already been made of the open-mindedness shown by William II and, in general, by all the Norman rulers, towards the various peoples that made up their kingdoms: this is a trait that is also reflected in the field of artistic creation. It can be seen in France, in England as much as in Italy, in Puglia, Calabria and naturally, in Sicily. Here, traces of architectural and decorative traditions of Byzantine and of Arab origin (the peoples that preceded the Normans in ruling the island) were certainly far more numerous once than they are today. The Arabs were involved in the political and economic life of the country, the Byzantines were fewer in number but the contacts between the Normans and Byzantine Art were renewed by the frequent Norman incursions into provinces of the Eastern Empire, during which many suppose that artists (and, in particular, mosaic workers) were carried off to be re-settled in Sicily. Thus, examining the chief architectural monuments that were erected on the island in Norman times one constantly encounters Arab and Byzantine influence. In Palermo, for example, the churches of St. Cataldo and of St. John of the Hermits are clearly influenced by Islam, as are too the palaces known as the Zisa (completed by William II), the

Cuba and the Cubula (begun by the same king). The frequent use of lancet and simple pointed arches, the propensity for linear decoration (arabesque), are also of Moorish origin, whereas a Byzantine contribution is apparent in certain details of the ground-plans of the Church of the Martorana and the Palatine Chapel as well as, extensively, in the mosaics. The mosaics that shimmer at Cefalù, at Palermo and in the opinion of no small number of scholars, here too, at Monreale, where, in effect, Greek influence had been predominant. (see further).

Norman eclecticism is also reflected in the architectural layout — fundamentally late-Romanesque — of the Cathedral of Monreale. Here, in effect, Latin elements are incorporated (the great nave cut by two sequences of columns) as well as Byzantine ones (the square-plan transept crossing which differs however from the Palatine Chapel and the

Church of the Martorana in that it is without a dome). Arab elements are the use of pointed-arch arcading, the conformation and decoration of the ceiling, newly restored today, supported on exposed and painted beams in the aisles and stylized stalactites in the crossing. Nor is there any lack of a more authentically Norman voice in this cosmopolitan language: the marked robustness of the structures and the placing of the two towers at the extremities of the west front. A Sicilian antecedent for the corner towers can be found at the Cathedral of Cefalù, that for majestic structure has most affinity with the Cathedral of Monreale even though at Cefalù the stylistic aspect is, on the whole, more markedly North-European. Unfortunately, the towers of Monreale were not finished, as has been said, and the south-west tower, deprived of its spire, has lost its primitive vitality: its heavy walls are lightened today only by

Plates 29 to 31: Central Apse.
At this point illustration of the cathedral mosaics commences, starting with the apse that is, liturgically speaking, the highest place in the temple. Dominating all from the conch is the Christ Almighty giving his blessing in Greek manner (Pl. 29). Beneath the Christ is the Madonna Immaculate with Child, flanked by two archangels and the apostles (Pl. 30). Along the lower fascia of the apse wall are the figures of 14 male and female saints. On the great arch before the apse the etoimasìa *is symbolized — the coming of Christ the Judge and Redeemer.*

30

34

35

Plates 32 to 35: *South-east apse and* diakònikon *walls. Stories of St. Peter.*

The space before the south-east apse is called diakònikon *because it was reserved to the deacons, just as the corresponding area before the north-east apse was called* pròtesis *because there, the rites to be celebrated were prepared. In the vault of the diakònikon is the bust of the Christ Emmanuel (from the Hebrew: God with us) framed by four cherubims or seraphims (Pl. 32). The Emmanuel is depicted as a beardless youth in accordance with ancient Byzantine iconographic tradition.*

In the conch of the apse stands out the enthroned figure of St. Peter, the prince of the apostles, blessing with his right hand and holding the Gospels and the symbolic keys in his left (Pl. 33). Surrounding St. Peter are representations of the significant moments of his life, among them The Fall of Simon Magus by the command of Peter and the prayer of Paul (Pl. 35) and the Crucifixion of St. Peter (Pl. 34).

36

37

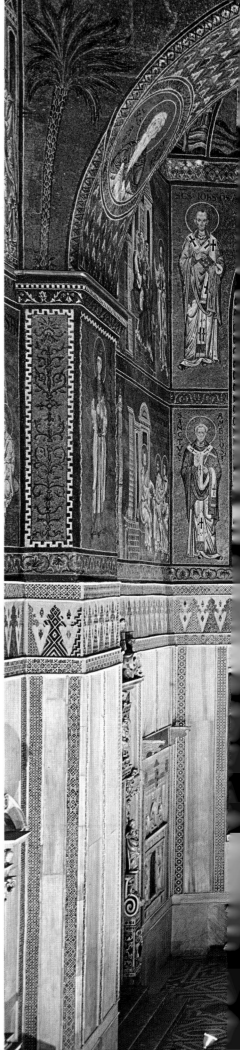

Plates 36 to 38: *North-east apse and pròtesis walls. Stories of St. Paul. "The preacher of truth and the people's teacher", as the Latin script says, appears in the same attitude as St. Peter in the conch of the north-east apse (Pl. 38). Among the stories of his life to be seen here is the* St. Paul delivering letters concerning the conversion of peoples to Timothy and Silas (Plates 36 and 37).

single-light apertures and on the upper floor by twin lights.

The artistic interest of the exterior of the church lies in the upper part of the west front and in the apses on which the decoration, of mixed Arab and Byzantine tastes, consists essentially of intersecting, blind, pointed arches. Our admiration goes principally to the imposing apses of a burnished gold tonality on which the complex and notwithstandingly harmonious play of the arches, of the miniature columns, of the rosettes and the horizontal fascias, is enriched by the inlay of limestone and lavic stone.

Two portals lead into the church. The main one is by far the more ornate with its delicate relief work and mosaic fascia surround: it dates from Norman times and was probably the work of the craftsmen who carved the capitals of the cloister (R. Salvini "Monreale e la scultura romanica in Sicilia", Palermo 1962; W. Krönig, "Monreale e l'architettura normanna in Sicilia", Palermo, 1965). One pauses before this portal to admire the 42 panels of the bronze doors sculpted by Bonanno Pisano· (signed and dated 1186), with reliefs that tell the stories of the two Testaments, from the *Creation of Adam* to *Christ Enthroned blessing the world*. The scenes show a freshness of invention that not unrarely achieves poetry: they are broadly modelled but charged with powerful emotion. The explanatory texts are in an abbreviated Latin that in one case (*Caim uccise frate suo Abel* / Cain kills his brother Abel) gives way to the growing Italian language. The style of these panels that, in the opinion of some, is redolent of the sculpture of the Rhine region, has, instead, been spoken of recently in connection with the coeval Pisan school that combines Byzantine and Provencal influences. The north front portal of the cathedral has bronze leafs signed by Barisano da Trani, in-

stalled here between 1186 and 1190. They are less significant artistically than those of Bonanno (whereas in the past they were more admired); here, the aims of the sculptor are primarily decorative and make frequent recourse to elements of Byzantine style. The leafs consist of 28 panels representing sacred scenes (the *Crucifixion,* the *Resurrection, Christ blessing,* the *Madonna Enthroned, Saints* – with the recurring effigy of *St. Nicholas of Bari* and *Apostles* etc.,) as well as mythological and symbolic scenes.

The interior of the cathedral is divided into three aisles — the central aisle being three times broader than the side aisles — terminating beyond the presbytery, in three semicircular apses. Separating the aisles are eighteen columns which, with one exception in cipolin marble, are all of ancient granite. The magnificent capitals that crown them (on which stand the mosaic covered pulvins — the structural supports of the arches) are partly decorated with figures, partly with ornamentation following classical schemes; they are of unknown origin but could date perhaps

from the early years of the Roman Empire. The pavement, fitted marble in the aisles and decorated with mosaic work in the

Plates 39 and 40: *The pròtesis walls.*

Plate 39: The disciples lower St. Paul from the walls of Damascus to free him from the hands of the Jews. Plate 40: Ananias the priest baptizes Saul who takes the name of Paul. *A ray from heaven bearing the Holy Ghost in the shape of a dove shines down on Paul. There is an extraordinary resemblance between these stories and the corresponding ones in the Palatine Chapel in Palermo.*

41

presbytery, dates from the XVI - XVII centuries with later interventions; the ceiling was almost entirely reconstructed after the fire of 1811. The levels of the temple,

Plates 41 and 42: *The* solea *walls. The mosaics of King William II. On the walls above the king's throne is a mosaic representing William II receiving the royal crown from Christ (Pl. 41). On the opposite wall, above the archiepiscopal throne, William, kneeling, offers a model of the cathedral of Monreale — here of entirely arbitrary form — to the Madonna, while God bestows his blessing on this act of dedication (Pl. 42).*

in altimetric sense (by steps) but also symbolically speaking, to denote a hierarchy of elevation, increase in height from nave to High Altar which, in point of fact, stands in the most exhalted space in respect of the pavement of the nave. Laterally, in the presbytery, is the solea that incorporates the seats reserved for the supreme political and religious authorities: the royal throne (to the left, facing the altar) and the archiepiscopal throne (to the right of it). The presence of a solea at Monreale continues a custom established in the churches of the Eastern Empire since the times of Paleochristian temples. The central apse is

flanked by two minor ones: the one on the right known as the diakònikon (from the Greek: place reserved for the deacons), that on the left the pròtesis (from the Greek: preparation) because it was here that the clergy gathered to prepare for the rites. Even the trilobed apse has a mystical significance in Byzantine planning: that of symbolizing the Divine Trinity.

As has been said, some chapels were incorporated into the temple that, although extraneous from their context stylistically, do not diminish its artistic interest, The most ancient is that of St. Castrense, protector of Monreale (1956), that the archbishop Ludovic II Torres had built, intending to be buried there himself (the entrance is from the south aisle). The burial did not take place here (the prelate's tomb is in fact in the church of St. Pancrazio, in Rome, where he died in 1609) but the founder of the chapel is, just the same, commemorated here by a marble statue that represents him kneeling in prayer, as well as by a painting by Pietro Antonio Novelli on the chapel wall facing the statue. Despite the recent modifications, the chapel retains its marked Renaissance stylistic character inspired by coeval Roman architecture. It is a rectangular space (today, of pronounced length), soberly decorated and broken only by a dome resting on a high tambour. Beneath this is the marble altar with the relics of St. Castrense — given to William II by the Archbishop of Capua — crowned by a dome-shaped baldacchino. Dating from almost a century later (1690) is the chapel of the Crucified Christ, built at the behest of Archbishop Giovanni Ruano whose tomb and commemorative statue are here (access is from the north transept). This chapel offers a splendid example of Sicilian Baroque that expresses with its elaborate articulation of forms

and blaze of coloured marble —
the so-called variegated marble —
a creative fantasy has nothing
gratuitous or capricious about it;
it is lucidly subordinated to the
purpose of creating an impression
of coherent and unitary volumes
(among the more illustrious
precedents for this chapel, see the
decoration of the church of St.
Catherine in Palermo). The chapel
was designed by Fra Giovanni da
Monreale but it is certainly the
great Jesuit architect Angelo Italia
of Licata (who replaced the
former in directing the building
and who was responsible for the
decoration of part of the church of
Jesus in Palermo) to whom we

must attribute the attainment of
an expression of such extreme
elegance, ennobled by the
meditated sacred character of the
imagery. A worthy introduction
to this sumptuous vision is the
richly carved portal with bronze
leafs decorated with tracery. The
plan of the chapel is hexagonal
and crowned with a dome; it is
clearly legible notwithstanding
the opulence of the sculptural
decorations (alluding to the
Passions of Jesus) alternating with
biblical inscriptions. The scene is
dominated by the tall tortile
columns and the four great statues
of the *Prophets* placed in niches:
those of *Daniel* and *Ezekiel*

Plates 43 to 46: *The south wing of
the transept. Stories of Christ.*
*In Pl. 43 can be seen the south walls
of this transept. From the stories il-
lustrated there can be seen here: the*
Transfiguration of Jesus on Mount
Tabor *and the* Resurrection of
Lazarus (pl. 44).
Jesus praying in the Garden of
Olives while the apostles sleep (pl
45), *the* Capture of Jesus *and the*
Kiss of Judas (pl. 46); *this latter is an
intensely dramatic composition that,
according to Bettini, is almost a
prefiguration of the style of Cimabue
at its most sovereign.*

44

45

modelled by Baldassare Pampillonia, those of *Isaiah* and *Jeremiah*, by Giovanni Battista Firrera: both Sicilian artists. Standing on the altar in veneration is the *Crucified Christ* (carved in wood in the first half of the fifteenth century) nailed, not to the Cross, but to the biblical Tree of Jesse: which signifies that the Crucifixion is a token of the Redemption foretold by the prophets. The chapel of the Crucified Christ leads to the cathedral. Particularly worthy of admiration, besides the magnificent cupboard delicately carved in wood by Trapanese artists are a staff, a monstrance, a silver ciborium and an illuminated parchment breviary of the fifteenth century.

The same Archbishop Ruano was responsible for the definitive organization of the lower part of the miniature side apses which as early as the sixteenth century had been converted into chapels in which can be seen the altar of the Sacrament (on the left) and that of the Madonna del Popolo (on the right): these too are Baroque works, probably from the hands of the same master craftsmen who worked on the chapel of the Crucified Christ, based on the use of variegated marbles, a technique that became popular in Messina during the first half of the sixteenth century. Above the altar of the Sacrament hangs a *Crucified Christ* from Rome, placed here by Archbishop Ludovic II Torres (1590); above the altar of the Madonna del Popolo is displayed in a niche a wooden statue of the *Madonna and Child*, possibly of the late fifteenth century. From the opposite side of the transept one enters the chapel of St. Benedict, founded in 1569 but arranged as it is to be seen today in the first half of the eighteenth century.

It too is an expression of Sicilian Baroque, but in its ultimate phase. The expressive timbre here, however, is quite different from

Plates 47 and 48: *The south wing of the transept.*

Pl. 47: *The* Entrance of Jesus into Jerusalem: *here too, just as with certain, of the stories of St. Paul, an analogy to the mosaics in the Palatine Chapel can be felt.* Pl. 48: Jesus before Pilate. *A boy sent by the wife of Pilate (who has had a premonitory dream) exhorting the Procurator of Judea to free Jesus.*

Plate 49: *The north wall of the north wing of the transept. Stories of Christ: The* Deposition from the Cross; *the* Placing in the Sepulchre; *the* Descent into Limbo; *the* Meeting by the Way to Emmaeus; *the* Supper at Emmaeus; *the* Disappearance of Jesus; *the* Disciples going to Jerusalem; *the* Miraculous Catch of Fish; *the* Ascension; *the* Pentecost.

Plates 50 to 53; *The north wing of the transept.*

Plate 50: *The* Supper at Emmaeus: *Christ offers the two disciples bread marked with a cross and is recognized by them.* Plate 51: *The* Ascension of Jesus *in the presence of the Madonna, the angels and the apostles.*

Plate 52: *The* Pentecost: *The rays of the Holy Ghost shine on the apostles gathered in the supper-room.* Plate 53: *The* Miraculous Catch of Fish: *Peter dives into the sea to worship the Saviour.*

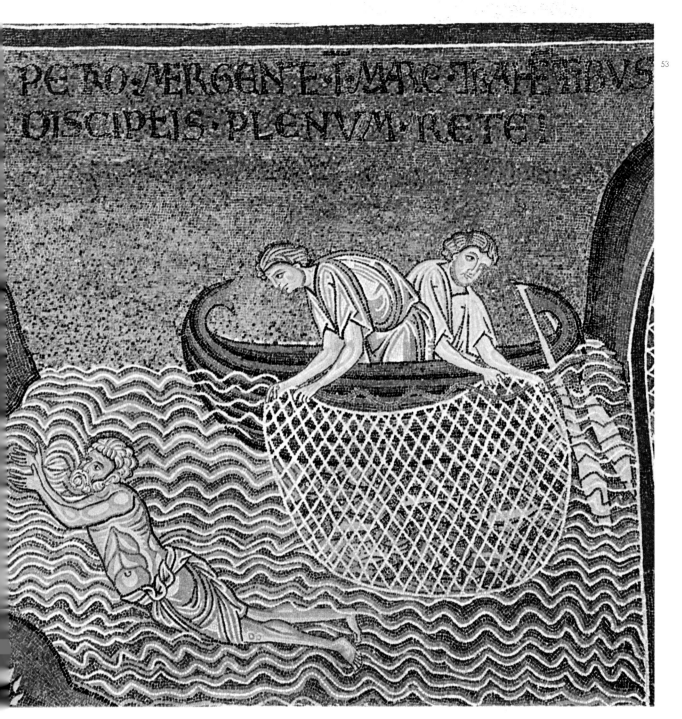

that of the chapel of the Crucified Christ. Here, in effect, vigorous decorative exuberance is replaced by a more controlled and simplified articulation of the ornamental elements within the architectonic space. It is lighter, a foretaste of Rococò and, in any case, a reminiscence of classicism (the nearest example is, in Palermo, the Oratory of St. Lawrence by Serpotta). The chapel is extremely luminous, the walls are faced with polychrone marbles of predominantly green and brown hue. Half-way up, inside panels, are ten *Stories of the life of St. Benedict*, carved in white marble: the author is Giovanni Battista Marino (1728). Higher up, other marbles and plaster-work (by Gaspare Guercio of Trapani), very light in tonality, enrich the decorative patrimony of the setting. Dominating all, from the altar is the *Glory of St. Benedict*, a masterpiece of the sculptor Ignazio Marabitti (signed and dated 1776) for the sensibility of its graduation of carved planes — beginning with the forceful relief of the figures of the Saint and the angels that carry him up to heaven and subsiding in the tenuous palpitations of the firmament furrowed by the rays of the Trinity and the nimbi that frame the joyful angels. In the chapel are the funerary monuments of Jacopo Bonanno (died in 1754) and of Francesco Testa (who died in 1773), this latter carved by the

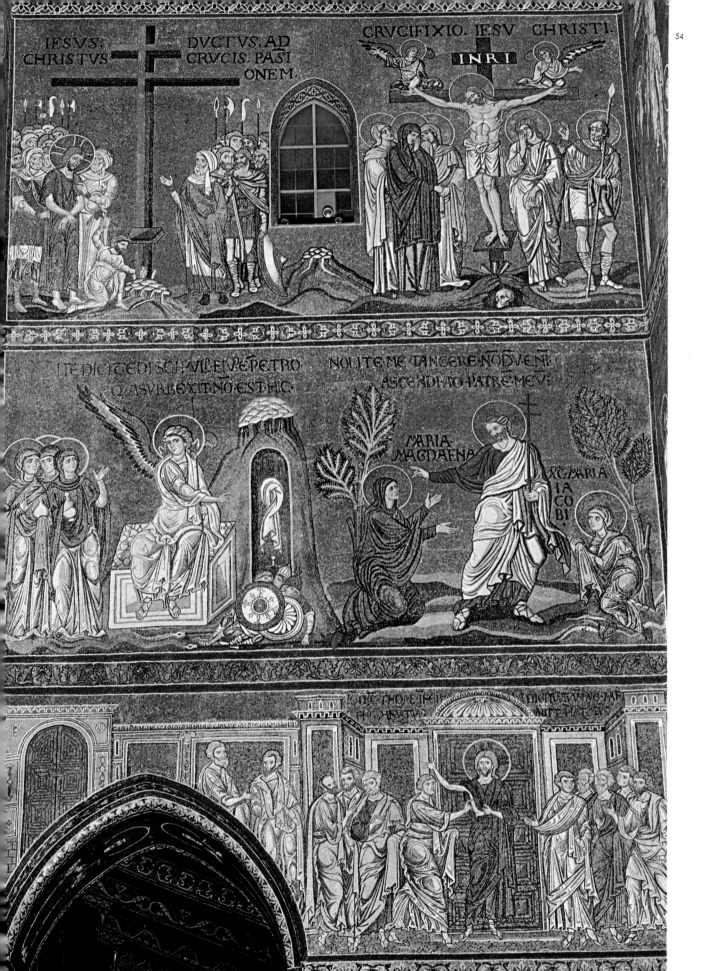

IESVS: CHRISTVS DVCTVS AD CRVCIS PASIONEM.

CRVCIFIXIO. IESV CHRISTI.

INRI

ITE DICITE DISCIPVLIS EVI(S) E PETRO Q(VI)A SVRREXIT NO(N) EST HIC.

NOLITE ME TANGERE NO(N)DVE(N)I(M) ASCENDI AD PATRE(M) MEV(M).

MARIA MAGDAENA

S(AN)C(T)A MARIA IACOBI

Plate 54: *The north wing of the transept. The west wall:* Jesus at the Foot of the Cross; The Crucifixion; *the* Pious Women at the Sepulchre; Jesus appears to Mary and Mary Magdalene; *the* Doubts of Thomas.

Plate 55: *Detail of the south wall of the central aisle. Stories from the Old Testament.*

aforementioned Marabitti (1775). Of the other works of art in the temple, only the most outstanding can be mentioned here: the High Altar, first and foremost, created in Rome by Louis Valadier (1770 - 1773), which miraculously survived the fire of 1811. It is inspired by late Roman Baroque and its quality — see the statues and reliefs in gold-plated silver and bronze — is fitting to the solemn purpose of glorifyng the Virgin to whom the temple is dedicated (bas-reliefs on the front of the altar), the Crucified Christ and the Saints particularly venerated at Monreale (St. Castrense, St. Benedict, St. Louis IX of France, St. Rosalia) that flank the figures of the two foremost apostles. Also to be seen in the church are: the sixteenth century bronze effigy of St. John the Baptist on a porphyry column (that originally supported

Plates 56 to 59: *The central aisle. South wall. Stories from the Old Testament.*
The mosaics of the two walls of the central aisle are dedicated to the stories from the Old Testament, from the Creation of the world *to the* Struggle between Jacob and the Angel. *The mosaic panels run along two fascia on each wall.*
The narration begins at the eastern extremity of the upper fascia of the south wall, proceeds along the reverse front, along the upper fascia of the north wall and the lower fascias of the south and the north walls.

Plate 56: God commences on the Creation of the World; Plate 57: *Detail of the* Creation of Light *in the presence of seven angels;* Plate 58: *Detail of the* Creation of the Earth separate from the Sea; Plate 59: *The* Creation of the Fish and the Birds: *peacocks, pheasants, skylarks, owls, pelicans and multicoloured fish in the waters of the Mediterranean create a scene of serene felicity*

OVCAT AQ. REPTIL E. AIE. VIVETI. 7 VOLA
E SVP. TRA. SVB. FIRMAM TO. CE LI

the baptismal font) in a niche faced with a mosaic representation of the baptismal font) in a niche faced with a mosaic representation of the Baptist (south aisle); two sar- William II (1575) in elegantly decorated light marble with reverent Latin inscriptions written by the Monrealese Antonio Veneziano (and placed here by the archbishop Ludovic I Torres who commissioned this monument) dedicated to William "cognomento Bono" (south transept). In conclusion, there is the monument-altar to St. Louis IX, King of France, which contains the relics of the Saint and a painting dedicated to him, by Giaconia, a Monrealese painter (north

transept) as well as the marble tombs of Margaret of Navarre, of Roger and Henry (rebuilt in 1846), the wife and sons of William I (in the same transept).

THE MOSAICS

The most famous works in the temple, the mosaics, were carried out with an overriding concern for the strict correlation between architecture and figuration. That is to say: the most symbolically sacred places in the temple (apse and presbitery) had to be dedicated to the most sacred mysteries of the Christian faith with stories of fundamental significance to the life of Christ and the foremost apostles while minor events connected with these mysteries, narrated in the Sacred

Scriptures were reserved for the remaining areas (the aisles). This real topographical hierarchy of imagery is typical of Byzantine mentality and it can be met with in other Norman churches in Palermo and in Cefalù. In all of these temples however, there are affinities in the figural balance of the mosaics although the balance is nowhere identical for various reasons: the conformation of the ground-plans, the scale of the area reserved for mosaics of al Monreale is the most extensive). as well as the intervention of benefactors in the choice and placing of certain subjects (for example: *Saints*). In the case in question, these were William II aided by the vice-chancellor Matteo d'Ajello, the English archdeacon Walter of the Mill and the Cluniae Benedictine monks.

The most exhalted place in the cathedral of Monreale is the conch of the apse, as at Cefalù, but not in the Palatine Chapel (in which it is represented by the dome of the sanctuary).

For this reason, at Monreale, the glorious multitude of semi-divine creatures (two wings of archangels, six wings of cherubims or seraphims and tetramorphs, the latter with four heads, symbolizing the four evangelists, the precursors of Christ (prophets), his disciples

Plates 60 to 62: *The central aisle. South wall (above).*

Plate 60: *The* Creation of Earthly Animals and of Man. *God gives Adam a soul by means of a ray that extends from the face of the Creator to that of Man.* Plate 61: God leads Adam to the Garden of Paradise *(paradise derives from the Greek* paràdeisos = *garden). The earthly paradise prefigures the celestial paradise.* Plate 62: Adam, alone. nourishes himself on the fruits of paradise.

62

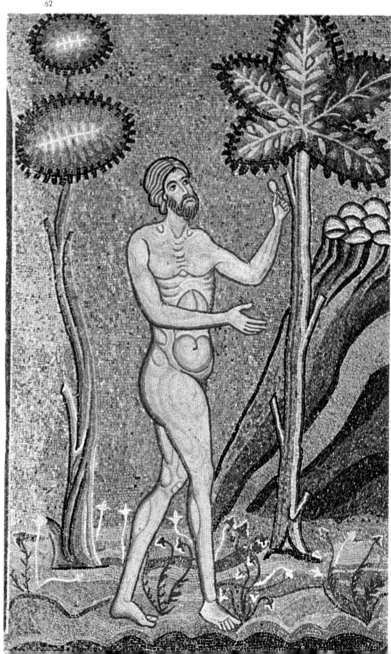

47

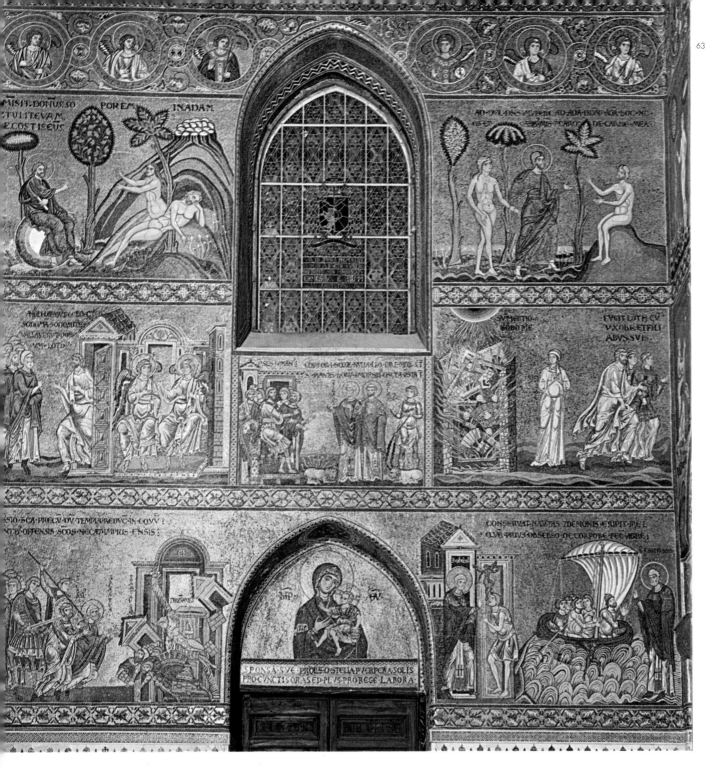

(apostles), his followers (bishops and saints) surround on every side the supreme apparition of *Christ Almighty* (from the Greek: Pantokràtor) in the conch of the central apse and of the *Miraculous Virgin Mother* (from the Greek: Panakràntos: the Wholly Immaculate) on the apsidal walls below.

Flanking the central apse, the two miniature apses commemorate the two principal apostles of the Church: Peter and Paul, by the evocation of the salient facts of their missions. Then, from the central section of the transept begins the Christological cycle (from the *Announcement to Zacharias* to the *Baptism of Christ*) that continues in the south transept (from the *Temptation of Christ* to the *Judgement of Pilate*), in the north transept (from the *Climb to Calvary* to the *Pentecost*) in the south aisle (from the *Heal-*

Plate 63: *The reverse front.*
Upper fascia: The Creation of Eve; Eve presented to Adam. *Middle fascia:* Lot and the Two Angels; *the* Destruction of Sodom.
Central panel of the middle fascia and lower fascia: Stories of the Saints Cassio, Casto and Castrense.
Lunette above the portal: the Madonna and Child "protectress of King William II".

Plate 64: *Central aisle. North wall (above): the* Original Sin.

48

R SVO OPS HOC SERPENTIS TVLIT DE FRVCTV
OMEDIT DEDIT VIRO SVO

ing of the daughter of the Woman of Cana to the Multiplication of the Bread and the Fishes) and in the north aisle (from the Healing of the Woman Bowed Down to the Healing of the Centurion's crippled son). The walls od the central aisle are dedicated to the events

Plate 65: *Detail of the north wall of the central aisle. Stories from the Old Testament.*

Plates 66 and 67: *The central aisle. North wall (above).*

Plate 66: The Expulsion from the Garden of Eden. *God reproves Adam and Eve for their sin and they cover their nakedness. The serpent gliding through the thorny acanthus bushes (symbol of tribulation) is crushed underfoot by God. Plate 67: The Punishment of the Ancestors. Adam is forced to work (here he is to be seen hoeing) while Eve meditates, afflicted, on the fate that awaits her. Fatigue and melancholy are imprinted on the faces of the condemned.*

CAYM·

ABEL.

DIX DS
FRIS TV

narrated in the Old Testament. Commencing with the upper fascia, north wall: from the *Creation of Heaven and Earth* to *Adam in the Garden of Eden*. Reverse front: the *Creation of Eve* and *Eve presented to Adam*. North wall: from *Eve tempted by the Serpent* to *Noah ordering the building of the Ark*. Continuing along the lower fascia, south wall:

Plates 68 to 70: *Central aisle. North wall (above).*

Plate 68: Cain kills Abel*: the story of humanity begins with fratricide, symbol of that violence that will stain the world with blood.* Plate 69: The Soul of Abel *(the small red figure)* asks for vengeance from God.

Plate 70: Blind Lamech pulls his bow and involuntarily kills the patriarch Cain. *Vengeance arrives through parricide.*

TRAHES LAMEC ARCV SVO ITFEC CAYM

DE·SCOM·DI·MANDATV·

CA·FAC·OPERARE·

OE·MISIT·COLVBA
REDIIT·CV·RAMO·
IVE

72

Plates 71 and 72: *Central aisle. South wall (below).*

Plate 71: Noah has the Ark built *in obedience to the command of God who has forewarned him of the Universal Flood. Workers are busy building the ark; on the right, two carpenters are sawing an enormous beam. The ark is crowned by a kind of tower with two windows.* Plate 72: *Detail of the Universal Flood: Noah extends his hand to receive the dove bringing an olive branch as symbol of the imminent end of the flood.*

55

CESSATO·DILVVIO·NOE EXTRA·HFECIT
BESTI·AS·AB ARCA·

from the *Building of the Ark* to *Abraham gives hospitality to the Three Angels*. Reverse front: *Lot and the Two Angels* and the *Destruction of Sodom*. North wall: *God commands Abraham to sacrifice Isaac* to the *Struggle between Jacob and the Angel* (see plan).

This is the scheme, in brief, of the mosaic-cycle of the temple. It is enriched by many other figure compositions however, particular-

ly in the apse-presbytery zone. Of these, there are the numerous evocations of Christ as the *Emmanuel* (from the Hebrew: God with us and, according to the symbolic significance, Christ judging at the end of the centuries: this is a figure of the young, beardless Saviour recalling the Apollo-like Christ of the more ancient Byzantine imagery); then, too, there is Christ the *Redeemer* (in the usual iconographic tradition, as a beard-

Plates 73 to 75: *Central aisle. South wall (below).*

Plate 73: Noah, the Flood ended, liberates the animals from the ark.

Plate 74: The Grape-harvest and the Drunkenness of Noah. *Noah, having drunk too much, falls asleep half-naked; his sons deride him and Cam covers his nakedness.* Plate 75: The Building of the Tower of Babel: *animated evidence of building procedures in Mediaeval times, directed by "Building Masters".*

74

75

FILII NOE · hEDIFICAN | | TES · TRICOFMSEST
QVE · EOITVOCATV · E | | LOCILLVO · BAB

ed man); the symbolic figuration of the preparation for the coming of Christ the Judge (from the Greek etòimasia: the Throne, the Cross and the signs of the Passion of Jesus), from the beginning of the Redemption (the *Annunciation to Mary,* from the Greek kairetismòs: greeting), of the Divine Passion (the veil with the visage of Christ, from the Greek mandylion), of the sacred *Logos* as the inspiration of the Creation (from the Latin: *Sapientia dei*). There are, as has been said, numerous complementary figures: angels, apostles, saints, bishops, evangelists, doctors of the Church, martyrs, hermits, deacons, prophets, paleotestamentary personnages. They are full-length figures in the apse-presbytery zone (see, especially, the apostles flanking the Immaculate Madonna and the male and female saints, in the fascia beneath, among them Thomas à Becket, canonized by Alexander III in the very reign of William II), except in the intradosses where they appear as busts within medallions. These busts continue along the fascia beneath the roof on the two wall of the central aisle and in the intradosses of the sequences of columns that delineate the aisles. A small story cycle on the reverse front recalls the Saints Cassio and Castro, and St. Castrense. Just as in the church of the Martorana at Palermo (where there is an effigy of Roger II) there is the portrayal of the founder of the cathedral, a presence that is clearly "political" in intent. William II appears twice on the walls of the solea: on the wall above the royal throne, in the act of being crowned king by Christ, and on the facing wall there, donating the cathedral of Monreale to the Virgin; this theme is treated once more on a capital in the cloister.

In conclusion, one should not overlook the decorative mosaic-fabric that serves as an interval of

76

77

luminosity and vivid colour between one figure composition and another: vases and floral garlands with the recurring motif of acanthus leaves decorate the extradosses of the arches of the colonnade; slim strips of ornamental geometric friezes, different one from another, gleam from the marble dado of the temple (like the tile decorations on the walls of Arab palaces) seeming almost to lap the extremity of a continuous fascia in which an un interrupted sequence of a single decorative element, inspired by the lily, runs from the reverse front to the apse. Other mosaics

shimmer from the embrasures of the windows while the floor of the presbytery offers a diversity of mosaic tesserae compositions and interwoven geometric patterns. Clearly, then, there is very little of the architectonic space of the temple that is not given over to mosaic, and the immense mosaic tapestry (comprising figure compositions and decorative elements) has an overall extension of about 10.000 sq. metres according to the most recent measurements: much more therefore than the 6,340 sq. metres usually indicated.

When were the Monreale mosaics carried out, and by whom?. We do

Plates 76 and 77: *Central aisle. South wall (below).*

Plate 76: Abraham meets the three angels sent by God and prostrates himself at their feet. Plate 77: Abraham invites the angels to dine at his table. *His wife, Sarah, listens incredulously to the prophesy of the imminent birth of a son.*

Plate 78: *Central aisle. North wall (below).*
The sacrifice of Isaac. *God, having commanded Abraham to sacrifice his son Isaac, sends an angel to stay the knife already in Abraham's hand.*

REBECCA·VADIT·CV·SERVO·A

REBECCA·

АНЕ

ESAV. HIC·BE AC·IACO

Plates 79 to 81: *Central aisle. North wall (below).*

Plate 79: The journey of Rebecca and the servant of Abraham. *The two, on camel back, ride towards the home of Isaac (son of Abraham) whom Rebecca will eventually marry.* Plate 80: *Detail of the* Blessing of Jacob. *Esau returns to his father Isaac with his kill.* Plate 81: *Detail of the* Flight of Jacob: *Rebecca exhorts her favourite son to flee to his uncle's house.*

IACOB·

61

VIDIT·IACOB·
SCĀA·SVMITĀ
EI'·CELO'
TANGEBAT·

IACOB·

EREXIT·IACOB·LAPIDE·IN
TITVLV·FVNDES·OLEV·

DESVP:

IACOB·

JACOB·FVGIC

Plates 82 to 84: *Central aisle. North wall (below).*

Plate 82: The Dream of Jacob. *On his way to his uncle's house Jacob falls asleep and dreams of a stair reaching up to God on which two angels are ascending and descending. On awakening Jacob erects a monument to God. Plate 83: Jacob continues on his flight. Plate 84: The Struggle between Jacob and the Angel. Jacob recognizes the angelic nature of the stranger. The angel then blesses him and bestows on him the new name of Israel: Jacob is the forefather of the Hebrew people.*

IACOB·LUCTAVIT·CU·ANGLO·
ANGLS·BENEDIC·ET·DICES·NO
A
CLOVA·VOCABIS·IACOB·S·ISRL·ERIT
NOM·TVV·

not know; as is the case with many ancient works. Scholars have therefore compared the work here (for iconography, style, decoration etc.,) with coeval and precedent mosaic work and painting in Sicily, in the Byzantine Empire, in Russian and Slav territory, in central-southern Europe and, in Italy, in Venice and in Rome. The results are, at least in part, divergent, even if on two points everyone is more or less in agreement: that the lay-out, as has been said, was conceived by a Byzantine mind (or in-

fluenced by one) and that the work began with the central apse. The massive bibliography on Monreale, dating from the end of the sixteenth century (Giovanni Luigi Lello) and comprising vast and ponderous volumes (such as the works of the aforementioned Gravina) is too voluminous to consent here to reference, however brief, to everything that has been written on the subject. Here, only a brief mention can be made of some of the viewpoints that seem to be of major interest.

Plates 85 and 86: *South aisle. Stories of Christ.*
The mosaics in the two aisles continue the stories of Christ begun in the central section of the transept. The sequence of the stories begins in the south aisle and continues in the facing one. Plate 85: *Detail of the* Ridding of Evil Spirits out of the daughter of the Woman of Cana: *the devil flees from the girl's mouth.* Plate 86: *The face of Christ. It is a detail from the* Healing, *at Capernaum, of the Dumb Man Possessed of Evil Spirits. Those possessed by evil spirits were, for the most part, epileptics.*

The reader is referred to personal consultation of the works that will be mentioned to acquire a clearer and more thorough knowledge of the matter. It must be said that for the first decade of this century (and also in the preceding one, with Gravina) and in 1946 with Di Pietro, the prevalent opinion was that the Monreale mosaics were almost entirely by local craftsmen who carried them out following on experience gained on earlier works in Sicily. Works that date, it must be underlined, to the late eleventh century (the church of Troina, where now nothing remains, being the matrix) when the Normans were not yet rulers of the island. Today, this hypothesis, although not rejected à priori, is viewed cautiously and subject to various distinctions.

At the present moment the stylistic evaluation of the mosaics of Monreale oscillates between two opposing poles: that of a prevalence of Byzantine or Oriental character (with regard to this, see the sumptuous volume of Ernst Kitzinger, "I mosaici di Monreale", Palermo, 1960), and that of a prevalence of Romanesque or Western character, this latter being the consequence of Venetian mosaic workers operating at Monreale (Roberto Salvini, "Mosaici medievali in Sicilia", Florence, 1949).

It is rather arduous to define these two contrasting concepts, of Byzantine character and of Romanesque character because neither the one nor the other offers fixed and absolute points to refer to, and still less points unvarying in time and place (however, any definition is always a synthesis). Both, in fact, (that is, both Byzantine and Romanesque art) follow tortuous, intricate paths that only in a few masterpieces culminate in a finality of style that consents to clarity of definition. With regard to this, Sergio Bettini admonishes that too rigid classification leads to abstractions, and for good measure, Cesare Brandi com-

Plates 87 and 88: South aisle.

Plate 87: *Detail of the* Healing of the Leper. *The sick man implores Jesus to aid him saying "If you wish to, O Lord, you can heal me".*

Plate 88: *Detail of the* Healing of the Man with a Withered Hand. *The mosaic representation suggests, in reality, a man suffering from deforming arthrosis or Dupuytren's disease.*

ments ironically on "latifondi stilistici" — stylistic compartmentalizing, having far too sharp a definition. This is valid for every artistic current, but in particular for whatever lies on the path between Byzantine art and Romanesque art. But a definition of the "idea" of Byzantine art and the "idea" of Romanesque art is necessary here, a synthesis that will throw light on the most characteristic qualities of both the one and the other, even though they be recognizable, as has been said, only in the most perfect achievements of the two styles. Let it be said then, with evident over-simplification, that Byzantine art reflects the tendency to reach an overall harmony by means of balance of linearity and colour, of single element and compositive whole, as well as by a propensity to conciliate the divine and the human in visions purified of any excess of externalized emotivity. In Romanesque art, on the contrary, the regard is turned firstly to reality and the man immersed in it, his concrete feeling and activity (think, for example, of the symbolic figurations of the *Months* with the terrestial activity connected to them, so frequent in Romanesque sculpture). As is well known, the creative orientation of Romanesque art was destined to mature and enrich itself over the course of centuries, above all on Italian soil. Consequently this art (in the case in question, painting) tends to offer, however crudely, the illusion of the three-dimensional quality of reality, in place of the eurythmic but almost abstract single-dimension Byzantine linearity.

But at Monreale there are no clearly defined distinctions between the declaredly Byzantine (Oriental) and the declaredly Romanesque (Western) but only stylistic elements that partake of both worlds, and this is coherent with the historical-artistic development of this place and

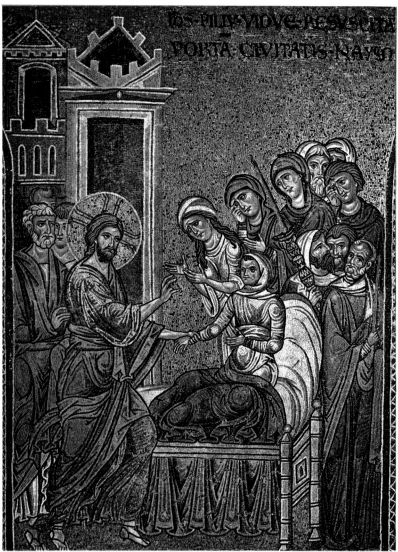

time. Thus, critical interpretation strives to enucleate from this mixture, at least some stylistic tendency, a prevailing "creative spirit". Without excluding, obviously, an infinite variety of nuances emerging from the comparison of each single work with what is presumed to be its model, whether clearly Byzantine or clearly Romanesque.

Very schematically then, it can be said that for Kitzinger, this model at Monreale, is the pictorial art that spread over the Eastern world during the reign of the last of the Byzantine emperors of the Commagene dynasty; for Salvini, it is to be sought in the mosaics of St. Mark in Venice, where, in fact, there was a confluence of Byzantine and Western-Romanesque stylistic influences but with, in ul-timate, a prevalence of the latter. Salvini's survey comprises the mosaics of Torcello, as well as those of St. Paul without the Walls and St. Peter in Chains (S. Paolo fuori le mura and S. Pietro

Plate 89 and 90: *South aisle.*

Plate 89: Jesus walking on the Waters. *The Redeemer approaches the disciples' boat, at the mercy of the tempest. St. Peter wishes to reach Jesus but his faith is lacking and he is about to drown when Christ saves him. The breakers that scourge the boat die down under the feet of Jesus.* Plate 90. The Resurrection of the Widow's son at the *Port of Nain.*

in Vincoli) in Rome, all executed by Venetian craftsmen (forerunner in this line of research is Sergio Bettini).

In the writings of both Kitzinger and Salvini the critical commitment is amply confirmed by an attentive and detailed examination of all the aspects of the problem but the conclusions, as has been said, diverge. Thus, for the former, at Monreale, one looks to the East, for the latter, to the West. The two scholars are not even in agreement over dates. In fact, for Kitzinger, the whole of the mosaic decoration of

Monreale was concluded in the period in which William II died, whereas for Salvini, on the contrary, the mosaics of the apse and the presbytery must have been terminated around 1189, those of the transept at the beginning of the thirteenth century, those of the aisles towards 1218, the mosaics of the central aisle towards 1230 and, in conclusion, the mosaics of the reverse front could only have been completed in the second half of the thirteenth century. Standing mid-way between Kitzinger and Salvini are Sergio Bettini and Stefano Bottari for whom the

decorative work at Monreale was begun by the Byzantines and concluded by the Venetians.

It must be remarked that the first to pronunce this opinion was Bet-

Plates 91 and 92: *South aisle.*

Plate 91: *The* Healing of the Woman suffering from Haemorrhages for 12 years. *Having spent all her worldly possessions in vain the woman finds her salvation in Jesus.* Plate 92: Jesus brings back to life the daughter of Jairus, *one of the elders of the Capernaum synagogue (detail).*

94

Plate 93: *South aisle.*
Detail of the Multiplication of the
Loaves and the Fishes.

Plates 94 and 95: *North aisle.*
Stories of Christ.

Plate 94: *Detail of the* Healing of the
Woman Bowed Down *(probably this
was another case of arthrosis). The
miracle takes place in the synagogue and on a Saturday (like
other miracles) arousing protest
from the ruler of the synagogue. But
for Christ there are no rest days from
charity.* Plate 95: *The* Healing of the
man suffering from Dropsy. *The
scene is further testimony (among
the most frequently quoted) of the
attention paid by the mosaic artists
(above all in the* Miracles of Christ)
*to the representation of Man as he
really is, in joy and in pain, for good
or for evil, in beauty and in ugliness.
Here too sickness is not disguised
(in lip service to an aesthetic
idealization), on the contrary, it is
underlined, in the swollen belly of a
probable victim of hepatic cirrhosis.*

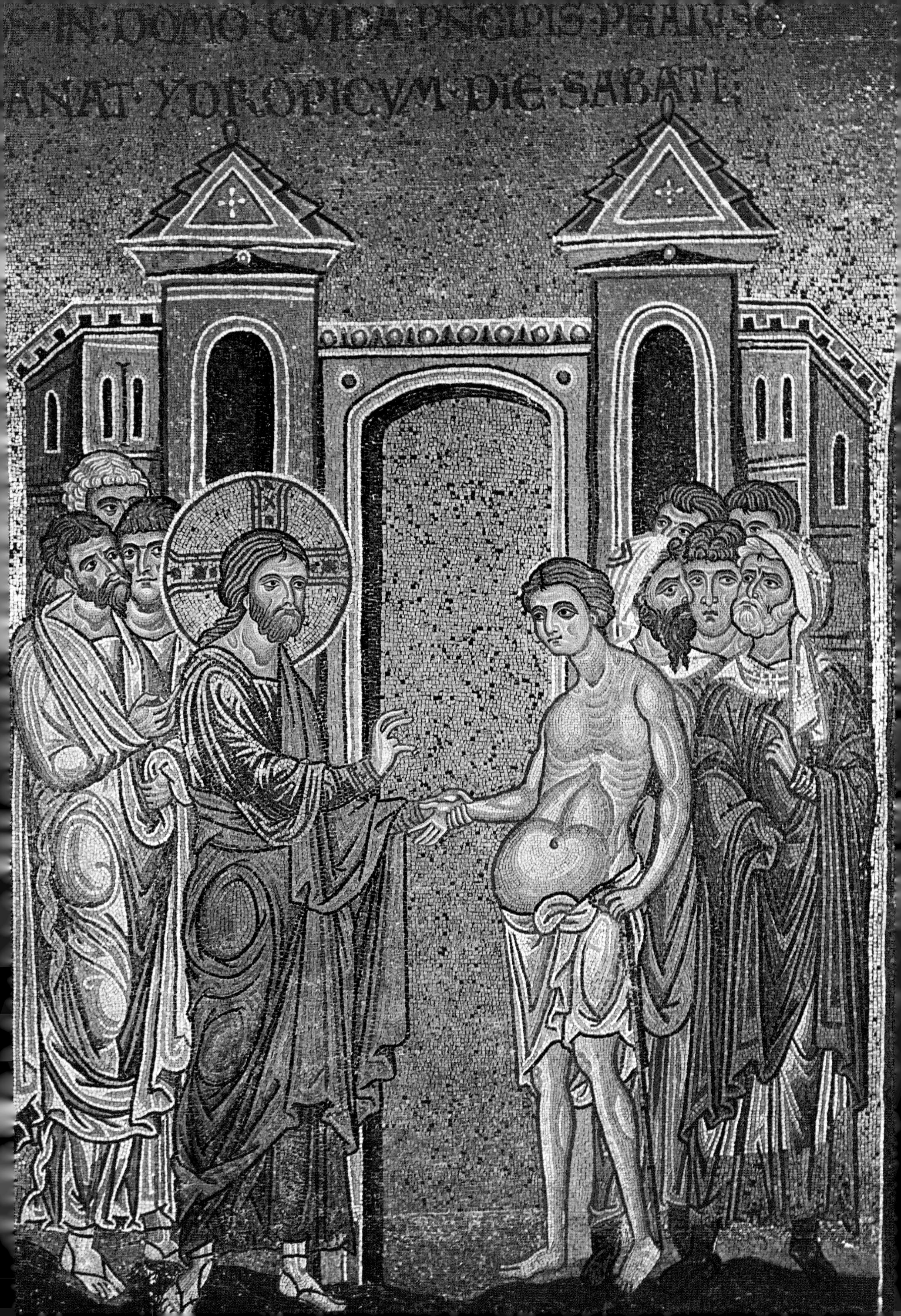
IN·DOMO·CVIDA·PNCIPIS·PHARISE
ANAT·YDROPICVM·DIE·SABATI

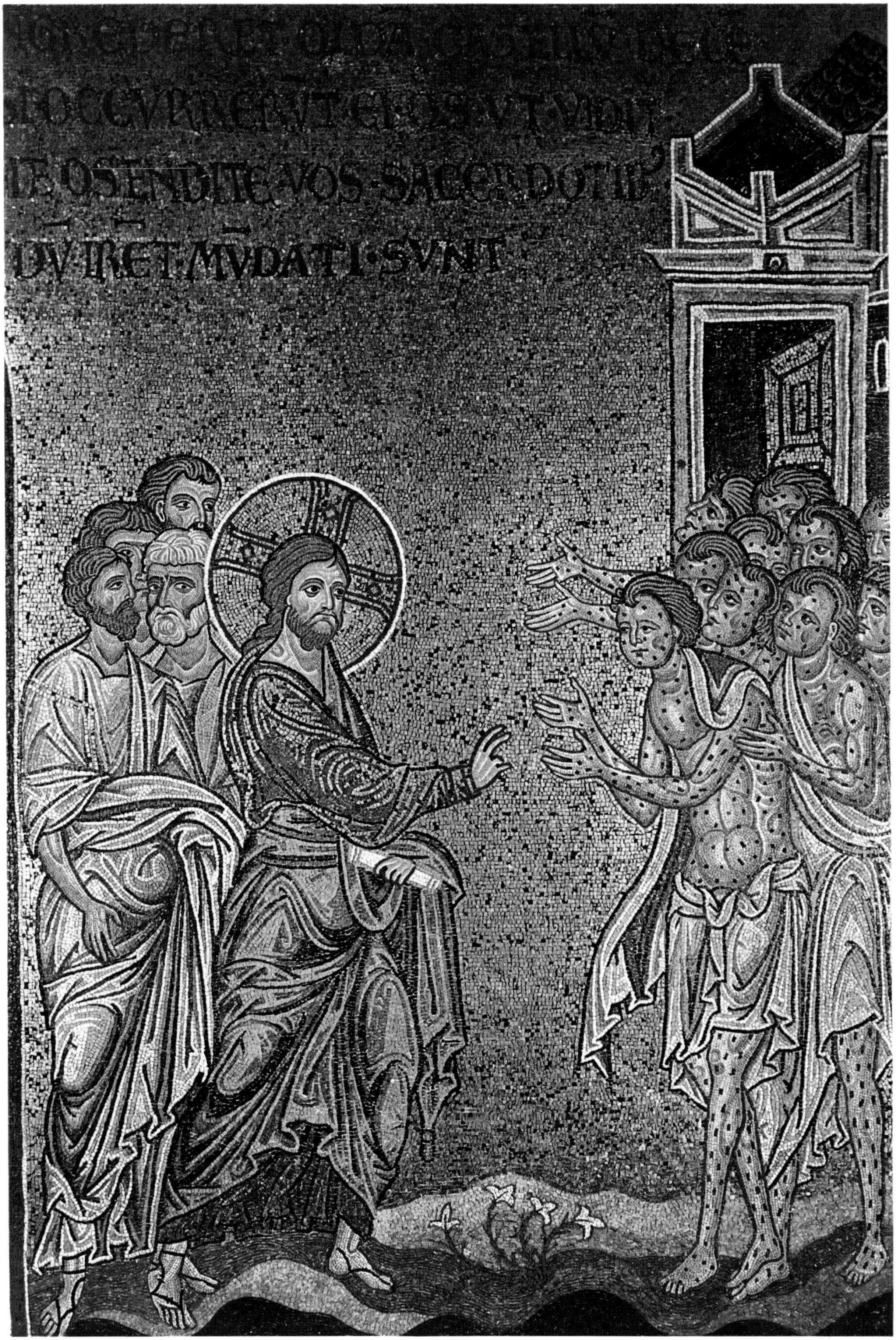
VOS SACERDOTIB
DV IRET MVDATI·SVNT

97

tini: ("La pittura bizantina. I mosaici", Florence, 1939); his subsequent "I mosaici di Monreale", Milano, 1969 being ulterior confirmation of it. Bettini's conclusion was taken up and examined by Stefano Bottari ("I mosaici della Sicilia", Catania, 1943) but here, only Bettini can be considered. The distinguished Byzantine scholar sees a stylistic dichotomy between the more ancient works (the Byzantine

mosaics of the apse and presbytery, terminated around 1189) and those of more recent date (the Venetian mosaics of the aisles and the reverse fronts, terminated not much earlier than the middle of the thirteenth century). In the older mosaics, there are echoes of Byzantine manner, due in part to the direct intervention of Byzantine craftsmen and in part to Sicilian artisans, heirs to the Byzantine tradition, while the later

mosaics bear witness to a stylistic struggle (a mixture of Byzantine and Western-Romanesque elements) which was taking place in Venice; a struggle, recognizable

Plates 96 and 97: *North aisle.*

Plate 96: Jesus healing the 10 Lepers. *The victims come out of a lazaretto with their hands extended imploring mercy.* Plate 97: *Detail of the* Healing of the Two Blind Men who proclaim their faith in Christ.

also in the previously mentioned fragments of Venetian mosaics existing in Rome.

On the overall aesthetic merit of the Monreale mosaics there are no great divergencies: it is generally admitted that the work, in itself gigantic, examined with a critical eye, denounces the prevalence of "routine" activity over creative tension. Whatever the stylistic tendency is considered to be at Monreale, the work of imitators has prevailed over that of innovators.

Some, like Kitzinger, direct attention above all to an exaggerated linearity (drapes, for example, so often depicted as if they were blown by the wind) deriving, though with attenuations, from late Commagene oriental models and, as there, lacking coordination to a whole, gratuitous, as well as narrow in colour range and devoid of musical consonance or dramatic effect. Others, like Salvini, concentrate on the effort to achieve three-dimensional quality (for example by emphatic high-lighting) and on the propensity to reduce the figuration to mere daily fact: observe, for example the *Stories of Christ* in the aisles, in which the humanity of the Redeemer and the imploring suffering of the afflicted, hoping to be healed by miracle, are immediately felt. As an example of accentuated figurative realism, the *Healing of the Man afflicted with Dropsy* and the *Healing of the Lepers* are frequently mentioned. There is no lack, in any of these scenes, of poetic intensity — particularly recurrent in certain of the *Episodes of the Passion of Christ* in the transepts (see, as examples, *Jesus praying in the Garden of the Jesus*; the two scenes of the *Deposition*; the *two Marys at the Sepulchre*; the *Nolite me Tangere* and in certain scenes from the *Expulsion from the Garden of Eden*; the *Work of Adam and the discomfort of Eve*; the *Drunkenness of Noah*; *Isaac asking Esau to bring back venison from the*

Plate 98: Jesus expells the descecrators from the temple. *Only in this scene does Jesus appear with his face marked with indignation. Discovering merchants in the temple, he overturns a money-lender's stall and expells cattle merchants and bird-sellers with a whip, shouting "You have transformed my house into a den of thieves". The sharp realism of the scene recalls the stories of Noah, the Tower of Babel and many other Miracles of Christ. Plate 99: Detail of the Forgiveness of the Adulteress. Jesus bends to write on the ground the sentence: "He who is blameless cast the first stone".*

hunt; Rebecca travelling with the servant of Abraham). For no-one today is the placing beside the mosaics of wording in Greek (central apse) and Latin (the remainder of the church) sufficient indication of the provenance of the craftsmen, even less an aid to reaching stylistic conclusions. The visitor who has already seen the Cathedral of Cefalù (for the mosaics in the apse) and those of the Palatine Chapel (for the mosaics representing *Testament Stories*) can compare them with those at Monreale for himself and thus weigh up the complexity of the problems that the scholar has had to face. And that are still to be resolved.

Plates 100 to 102: *North aisle.*

Plate 100: *Another detail of the Forgiveness of the Adulteress. The sinner shows by her contrition that she deserves divine clemency.*

Plate 101: *The* Healing *of the Paralytic. The sick man is lowered down from a specially made opening in the roof.* Plate 102: Mary Magdalene, *as a sign of contrition, anoints and washes with tears the feet of Christ who forgives her. Tle Apostles seated at table are amazed at this new teaching of love.*

THE CLOISTER

The artistic interest of the cloister is no less than that of the cathedral. It is an extremely harmonious, perfectly square loggia, each side 47 metres long. As in the church, the arches are of Arab style, graceful ogives, surmounted by a double hood-mould, within which there is the decorative diachromatic play of alternating limestone and lavic stone inlay. This same diachromatic ornamentation (which echoes that of the upper part of the west front and the apses) is repeated with variations, on a fascia beneath the roof. The whole, like a wind-borne melody, recalls the most delicate Moorish inventions. A cordon, unrelated to the structural context, resting on the abacuses of the capitals, protrudes from the intradosses of the arches. This addition has aroused a number of hypotheses, among the most recent that of Krönig who suggests that wooden slats were once fixed to this cordon, linking up the miniature columns and thus protecting the loggia from the summer heat or from the rigours of winter. In other words, an "amenity" for the Benedictines strolling around in the intervals between duties. The miniature columns that support the arches are of incomparable elegance, here, smooth, there, decorated or inlaid with a mosaic facing that changes from column to column with unfailing fertility of invention. The columns, 228 of them in all, are grouped in pairs along the sides, in fours at the corners. In the south-west corner of the cloister there is a loggia in miniature, the so-called "chiostrino" or "lesser quadrangle", in the centre of which a graceful column serves as the shaft of a fountain from which spouts the water contained in a sunken bath. It is the "king's fountain", so called because William II is said to have furnished the cloister with water: it is a place

103

that repeats the magic of a *patio* in Granada. Between columns and arches are the solid, massive capitals. Here the eye is lost in a forest of images. One is confronted with a sculptor's encyclopaedia — the richest in Sicily in view of the grave deterioration of the cloister of the cathedral of Cefalù. It gives one an idea of the vastity of the Mediaeval world of figurative, decorative and symbolic imagery. On certain capitals can be recognized ornamental motifs inherited from the classical world — in particular, the Corinthian and composite style — but often, more complicated, interlaced, almost metamorphosed by the addition of symbolical allusions. Carved on other columns are scenes evoking stories or figures from the Testaments — or, in some cases, pagan ones — some concerned with three-dimensional relief, others with affable story-telling. Everywhere, the eye has turned with passion to nature — vegetal, animal and human nature. There is also nakedness, presented with an emphasis that would seem out of place in the Christian world (in the cathedral, only the Progenitors are naked, but modestly so); there are scenes of everyday life; acrobatic displays; hunting, jousting, vine-harvesting and so forth. An extraordinary germination of motifs that shows no concern for the most bizarre associations.

The scholar's eye has tried to unravel this tangle and has traced the source for many apparently gratuitous representations to late-

Plates 103 and 104: *Two sides of the cloister of the monastery of Monreale.*

The construction of the convert was more or less contemporary with that of the cathedral and dates, according to prevalent opinion, to Norman times. However the only building that conserves its original aspect intact is the cloister and it is certainly the most beautiful building. Here, as in many cloisters, a profound serenity reigns supreme, suggested perhaps by the geometrical spatial perfection of the square arcade, softly broken by the curves of the arches supported on elegant miniature columns. In addition to the fascination of the setting, this cloister is of the highest artistic interest.

Roman bestiaries and, above all to Christian symbolism, whether of the West or the East. Viewed in this way, for example, the lion, the eagle, the calf, the lamb, the ram, the hippogriff, the grape, the ear of corn, all refer in various ways to Christ, while the thorn, the serpent and certain monstrous associations allude to the devil or to sin. Silence reigns as to dates and names. One remains, on a capital on the North side (XIX arch): that of a certain Romanus, son of Constantine the marble - worker, one of the tablet carvers of the cloister rather than a master craftsman (if Salvini's hypothesis is true), but the information reveals nothing.

With regard to the capitals as a whole, only those that tell a story or that follow a theme will be examined here. These capitals do not follow a topographical scheme

as do the cathedral mosaics: they alternate casually with other, purely ornamental or symbolical ones. This brief tour begins by proceeding straight ahead from the entrance to the cloister.

NORTH SIDE

Capitals of the VIII arch (*The parable of Dives*): Lazarus the beggar; Lazarus ejected by the servant of Dives; the death of Dives; the Soul of Lazarus in Abraham's lap; Dives in Hell. Capitals of the XIV arch (*Stories of St. John the Baptist*): Christ before the Pharisees; the Baptism of Christ; the Dance of Salome; the Decapitation of St. John the Baptist; the Baptist reproves Herod Antipator for his adultery. Capitals of the XXI arch (*Stories of Samson*): Samson kills the lion on his way to meet the Philistine woman; Samson sets the riddle

Plates 105 and 106: *Capitals in the cloister.*
The capitals of the cloister of Monreale offer the richest documentation of Mediaeval sculpture existing in Sicily. Their style has recently been linked by Salvini to the Romanesque sculpture of Provence.

Plate 105: The Evangelist Mathew, *flanked by a mermaid. On the sides, two symbols of the evangelists.* Plate 106: William II offers the cathedral of Monreale as a gift to the Virgin. *Observe that the little model of the cathedral has been inspired by the appearance of its south front.* Plate 107: *A view of the delicious "lesser quadrangle" built into the southwest corner of the cloister. In the centre of this little arcade, a miniature column forms the shaft of a fountain. Tradition has it that King William himself brought the water to this place.*

for the two Philistines; the Massacre of the Philistines; Samson flees from Gaza after having torn down the doors; Samson blinded in his sleep; Samson makes the columns of the temple tremble ("Samson dies with all the Philistines).

Capitals of the XXIV arch (*The Massacre of the Innocents*): Herod orders the massacre; two soldiers in conversation; the Massacre of the Innocents; the killing of the child in its mother's arms; the mother lamenting.

Capitals of the XXV arch (*the symbols of the four Evangelists and monks*). NORTH-EAST CORNER (*The Annunciation and the Nativity*): the Annunciation; Elizabeth embraces Mary (the Visitation); the announcement to Joseph; the Birth of Jesus; the Adoration of the Shepherds; the Journey and Adoration of the Three Kings.

EAST SIDE

Capitals of the XVIII arch (*Stories of Joseph the Patriarch*): the Dreams of Joseph, twelfth son of Jacob; Joseph tells his dreams to Jacob and to his brothers; Joseph visits his brothers grazing their animals; Joseph is thrown into the well by his hostile brothers; Joseph's brothers sell him to merchants who take him by camel to Egypt; the Desperation of Jacob on seeing the bloodstained clothes of Joseph. Capitals of the XX arch (*The Original Sin and its first consequences*): The Original Sin; Adam and Eve expelled from the Garden of Eden; the Progenitors condemned to work and suffering; the sacrifices of Cain and of Abel; the Murder of Abel; Lamech kills Cain.

Capitals of the XXIV arch (*After the Resurrection of Christ*): the Three Pious Women at the Sepulchre of Christ; Christ descends into Limbo; "Christ and the Magdalene".

SOUTH-EAST CORNER (*The Legend of the True Cross*): St.

Helena and Constantine show the True Cross discovered on Calvary beneath the Temple of Venus; the symbolic triumph of the Church over the Synagogue; the Queen of Sheba (worshiping the True Cross) and a cup-bearer (?); Figures of the Prophets.

SOUTH SIDE

Capitals of the XXII arch (*The Sacrifice of the Bull*): on the east side of the capital is a figure of a young man killing a bull. The scene alludes to the Oriental cult of the god Mithras (personification of the sun) that continued for some time in the West even after the conversion to Christianity. Mithras (wearing a Phrygian cap) killing the bull is the iconographic symbol of this religion. On the other sides of the capitals are ornamental motifs and figures.
SOUTH-WEST CORNER (both of the cloister and the "lesser quadrangle") (*The Apostles and Stories of Christ*): the Apostles urged by the angels to evangelize the world; the Pentecost; the Presentation of Jesus at the Temple; an apostle and Mary; the Flight into Egypt.

THE LESSER QUADRANGLE - NORTH-EAST CORNER (*Allegories of the Months*); January: an old man warming himself by a fire; February: pruning a tree; March: the horn player; April: gathering flowers; May: a horse at pasture; June: gathering fruits; July: harvesting corn; August: preparation of the vats; September: treading the grapes; October: sowing; November: gathering acorns; December: pig killing.

WEST SIDE

Capitals of the VI arch (*The Prophets*): Isaiah, Jeremiah, Daniel and David; the Annunciation and a centaur.
Capitals of the VI arch (*The Dedication of the Cathedral of Monreale* and Allegories):

William II dedicates the cathedral of Monreale to the Madonna (the scene repeats that of the mosaics in the cathedral but here, the model of the cathedral, diversely from in the mosaic representation seems to draw on the real aspect of the south front of the church); Justice, Charity, Faith and Hope; The Lamb of God.

Capitals of the XX arch (*Stories of Noah*): Noah, having left the Ark, sacrifices to God; the "Rainbow pact"; the three sons of Noah go to the vineyard and harvest the grape; Noah treads the grapes; the Drunkenness of Noah; Noah curses Cam; the Tower of Babel.

Capitals of the XXI arch (*The Prophets and the Madonna and Child*).

Capitals of the XXVI arch (*Stories of Jacob*): Isaac cheated by Rebecca and Jacob; Esau offers Isaac game; the Flight of Jacob; the Dream of Jacob.

Until recent times the predominant opinion concerning the stylistic character of these capitals was that they were influenced by coeval classical-influenced Campanian sculpture. This is the view of Adolfo Venturi ("L'arte romanica", Milan, 1904), Pietro Toesca ("Il Medio Evo", Turin, 1929) who, hower, does not exclude reminiscences of other Southern Italian cultures, and Stefano Bottari ("Storia dell'arte italiana", vol. I Milan-Messina, 1955) to whom it is illuminating to compare the Monrealese capitals and the church of St. Restituta in Naples and the atrium reliefs in the cathedral at Sessa Aurunca. Raffaele Delogu ("Sicilia", vol. I Milan, 1962) following a different interpretative path, accepts that besides the Campanian master craftsmen, artists of French origin (Ile de France) have intervened, however sporadically, in the cloister.

Roberto Salvini's monumental monography on the cloister of Monreale and Romanesque sculpture in Sicily (Palermo 1962) takes up the stylistic question again, "ab imis", analyzing each capital and comparing it with other works of the period in South Italy and in France.

Plates 108 to 114: *Capitals in the cloister.*

Plate 108: The Death of Dives and Lazarus ejected by Dives's servant.

Plate 110: *A capital with the figure of an acrobat.* Plate 111: The Annunciation, *among the most poetic sculptures in the cloister.* Plate 112: The Visit of Mary to Elizabeth *and* The Angel appears to St. Joseph. Plate 113: Samson asks a riddle of the two Philistines and imparts the solution to his wife; *the* Massacre of the Philistines. Plate 114: The Sacrifice of the Bull: *an evocation of the Oriental cult of Mithras.*

SANSON

The critic reaches the conclusion that even if the iconographic repertory of the cloister of Monreale has its roots in classicism and Byzantium (as is, for the rest, always the case in Mediaeval Europe), the pervasive "spirit" is decisively Western Romanesque. This "spirit" was infused in the body of the sculptural work in the cloister by craftsmen closely linked with Provencal art of that period. Salvini compares, in particular, the Abbey of St. Gilles, the facade and cloister of St. Trophime at Arles, and some pieces in the Calvet museum at Avignon. He has no doubts about the relation between Monreale and Campanian sculpture (in which he senses a Provencal influence) but he does not exclude that the influence may be inverse and, consequently, also the dating: that it stems in fact, from Sicily. Salvini's interpretive hypothesis is strengthened by the recognized importance and widespread diffusion of Provencal culture at that time, not only in the field of the figurative arts (consider, for examples the sculpture of the Comasque diocese) but also in that of linguistics and literature. The critical vision of the Author concludes with attributions by groups of works of the corpus of sculpture at Monreale. There were, working contemporaneously on these works, a number of master craftsmen (indicated by conventional names), the creators of the more mature artistic works, aided by collaborators and tablet carvers whose presence is felt by a certain decline in quality. With regard to the dating (approximately estimated) of the work (cloister and capitals), some critics tend to push it forward to within the first decade of the thirteenth century. The majority, like Salvini himself, tend to keep it to the years (around 1175-1189) in the course of which William II died.

BIBLIOGRAFIC NOTE

G.L. Lello, *Historia della Chiesa di Monreale*, Roma, 1595.

M. Del Giudice, *Descrizione del Real Tempio e monastero di S. Maria Nuova in Monreale*, Palermo 1702.

D. Pietrasanta di Serradifalco, *Del Duomo di Monreale*, Palermo, 1838.

D.B. Gravina, *Il duomo di Monreale*, vol. II - testo - Palermo, 1858-1859.

G. Di Marzo, *Delle belle arti in Sicilia*, II, Palermo, 1859.

A. Venturi, *Storia dell'arte italiana, Il Romanico*, Milano, 1905.

F. Gregorovius, *Passeggiate per l'Italia*, Roma, 1909.

C. Concetti, *Monreale e i suoi dintorni*, Palermo, 1912.

P. Toesca, *Storia dell'arte italiana, Il Medioevo*, Torino, 1929.

E. Mauceri, *Il Duomo e il Chiostro di Monreale*, Milano, 1929.

P. Muratov, *La pittura bizantina*, Roma s.d.

E. Diez-O.Demus, *Byzantine Mosaics in Greece*, Cambridge Maa., 1931.

F. Pottino, *Mosaici e pitture nella Sicilia normanna*, 1932.

C. Diehl, *La peinture byzantine*, Paris, 1933.

S. Bettini, *L'architettura bizantina*, Firenze, 1937.

S. Bettini, *La pittura bizantina, I mosaici*, Firenze, 1939.

S. Bottari, *I mosaici della Sicilia*, 1943.

S. Bettini, *La scultura bizantina*, Firenze, 1944.

F. Di Pietro, *I mosaici siciliani dell'età normanna*, Palermo, 1946.

S. Bottari, *L'architettura della contea, Catania*, 1948.

R. Silvini, *Mosaici medievali in Sicilia*, Firenze, 1949.

S. Bottari, *L'architettura della contea*, Catania, 1948.

R. Salvini, *Mosaici medievali in Sicilia*, Firenze, 1949.

S. Bottari, *Storia dell'arte italiana*, I, Milano, Messina, 1955.

E. Kitzinger, *I mosaici di Monreale*, Palermo, 1960.

S. Bottari, *L'arte in Sicilia*, Messina-Firenze, 1962.

R. Delogu, *Sicilia*, I, Milano, 1962.

R. Salvini, *Il chiostro di Monreale e la scultura romanica in Sicilia*, Palermo, 1962.

S. Bottari, *I mosaici bizantini in Sicilia*, Milano-Messina, 1963.

W. Krönig, *Il duomo di Monreale e l'architettura normanna in Sicilia,* Palermo, 1965.

J.J. Norwich, *I normanni nel Sud*, Milano, 1967.

P. Sébilleau, *La Sicilia*, Bologna, 1968.

S.F. Romano, *Breve storia della Sicilia*, Torino, 1970.

S. Correnti, *Storia della Sicilia*, Milano, 1972.

INDEX

GROUND-PLAN OF THE CATHEDRAL OF MONREALE WITH INDICATIONS OF THE SEQUENCES OF THE MOSAIC CYCLE.

CATHEDRAL

A — PORTAL BY BONANNO PISANO
B — PORTAL BY BARISANO DA TRANI
C — CHAPEL OF ST. CASTRENSE
D — CHAPEL OF ST. BENEDICT
E — CHAPEL OF THE CRUCIFIELD CHRIST
F — TREASURY

MOSAICS

C — CENTRAL APSE AND ADJACENT WALLS
CONCH OF THE APSE: Christ Almighty.
APSE WALL AND ADJACENT WALL: in the centre, the Immaculate Madonna with Child; at the sides, the archangels Michaek and Gabriel and the apostles (according to Byzantine classification) Peter, Paul, James the Little, Andrew, John the Baptist, Mathew, Luke, Mark, Bartholomew, Thomas, Philip, Simon.
Lower fascia: The Saints, Pope Clement; Pope Sylvester; Peter, Patriarch of Alexandria; Thomas à Becket, Archbishop of Canterbury; Stephen the Martyr; Deacon Laurence; Martin of Tours; Nicholas of Bari; Blaise of Sebaste; Hilary of Poitiers; Anthony of Thebaid; Benedict of Norcia; Agatha of Catania; Mary Magdalene.

STORIES OF CHRIST
H - TRANSEPT - CENTRAL SECTION (SOUTH - WEST - NORTH)
Upper fascia — 1. The Angel tells Zacharias that Elizabeth has conceived. 2. Zacharias leaves the temple. 3. The Annunciation. 4. Mary visits Elizabeth. 5. The Nativity. 6. The Magi and the Star. 7. The Three Kings offer gifts to Jesus. 8. Herod orders the Massacre of the Innocents. 9. The Massacre of the Innocents.
Lower fascia — 10. Joseph dreams of an Angel that advises him to flee to Egypt. 11. The Flight into Egypt. 12. The Presentation of Jesus at the Temple. 13. Jesus before the Elders. 14. The Marriage at Cana. 15. The Baptism of Jesus.

I - TRANSEPT - SOUTH WING (FROM SOUTH TO WEST)
Upper fascia — 1. Satan tempts Jesus to change stone into bread. 2. The temptation of Jesus on the summit of the temple. 3. Satan offers Jesus wealth in exchange for adoration. 4. The Healing of the Cripple at the Well. 5. The Blind Man healed by the Pool of Siloam.
Middle fascia — 6. Jesus and the Samaritan at the well. 7. The Transfiguration of Jesus on Mont Tabor. 8. The Resurrection of Lazarus. 9. The two disciples bring Jesus the ass and its colt. 10. The Entry of Jesus into Jerusalem. 11. The Last Supper.
Lower fascia — 12. The Washing of the apostles' feet. 13. Jesus praying in the Garden of the Olives while the apostles sleep. 14. The Taking of Jesus and the Kiss of Judas. 15. Jesus before Pilate.

L - TRANSEPT - NORTH WING (FROM WEST TO NORTH)
Upper fascia — 1. Jesus conducted to the foot of the Cross. 2. The Crucifixion. 3. The Deposition. 4. The Placing in the Holy Sepulchre. 5. Jesus Arisen, descends into Limbo.
Middle fascia — 6. The Pious Women at the Tomb. 2. Jesus appears to Mary and Mary Magdalene. 8. Jesus and his two disciples on the road to Emmaeus. 9. The Supper at Emmaeus: Jesus offers the two disciples bread marked with the Cross. 10. Jesus disappears, leaving the two disciples alone. 11. The two disciples go to the refectory in Jerusalem.
Lower Fascia — 12. The Incredulity of Thomas. 13. The Miracle of the Fish. 14. The Ascension of Jesus. 15. The Pentecost.

M - SOUTH AISLE (FROM SOUTH TO WEST)

1. Jesus ridding the daughter of the Woman of Cana of evil spirits. 2. The Healing at Capernaum of the Dumb Man possessed of evil spirits. 3. Jesus heals the Lepers. 4. The Healing of the Man with the Withered Hand. 5. Jesus walks on the waters and saves Peter. 6. The Raising of the Widow's son at the port of Nain. 7. The Healing of the Woman afflicted with Haemorrhages. 8. The Resurrection of the daughter of Jairus, Ruler of the synagogue. 9. Jesus cures the mother in-law of Peter of a fever. 10. The Multiplication of the Bread and the Fishes.

N - NORTH AISLE (FROM WEST TO EAST)

1. Jesus heals the Woman Bowed Down and reproves the ruler of the synagogue. 2. The Healing of the Man Afflicted with Dropsy. 3. The Healing of the Ten Lepers. 4. Jesus gives the two Blind Men their sight back. 5. Jesus expells the Desecrators from the temple. 6. Jesus forgives the Adultress. 7. A paralytic, lowered from the roof, is healed by Jesus. 8. The Healing of the Crippled and the Blind. 9. Mary Magdalene anoints and washes the feet of Jesus with tears. 10. The Healing of the Centurion's crippled son.

Jesus and his two disciples on STORIES OF ST. PETER

O - SOUTH APSE - LUNETTES AND DIAKONIKON WALLS

Conch of the Apse: 1. St. Peter enthroned. Lunettes and walls: 2. The angel appears to St. Peter in prison. 3. St. Peter, freed from prison, follows the angel. 4. St. Peter and St. John heal a cripple. 5. Aeneas the Paralytic healed by St. Peter. 6. St. Peter raises Tabitha from the dead. 7. The meeting of St. Peter and St. Paul in Rome. 8. The dispute between St. Peter and St. Paul and Simon Magus. 9. The Fall of Simon Magus. 10. The Crucifixion of St. Peter.

STORIES OF ST. PAUL

P - NORTH APSE - LUNETTES AND PROTESIS WALLS

Conch of the apse: 1. St. Paul enthroned. Lunettes and walls: 2. Saul receives letters for Damascus. 3. Saul, thrown down from his horse and blinded, is converted to the Christian faith. 4. The Three Wayfarers accompany the blind Saul to Damascus. 6. Ananias baptizes Saul, who takes the name of Paul. 7. The dispute between St. Paul and the Judges. 8. The Flight of St. Paul from Damascus. 9. St. Paul gives letters concerning the conversion of people to Timothy and Silas. 10. The Decapitation of St. Paul.

4. Rebecca travelling with the servant of Abraham. 5. Isaac sends Esau to hunt. 6. Isaac gives his blessing to Jacob. 7. Rebecca induces Jacob to flee. 8. Jacob dreams of a ladder reaching to Heaven. 9. The struggle between Jacob and the Angel.

STORIES OF THE SAINTS CASSIO, CASTO AND CASTRENSE

R - REVERSE FRONT - CENTRAL AND LOWER FASCIAS

Central Fascia — 2. The Saints Cassio and Casto condemned to be thrown to the lions that crouch at their feet.
Lower Fascia — 1. The Saints Cassio and Casto bring down the Temple of Apollo. 2. (Lunette) The Madonna and Child.
3. Two Miracles of St. Castrense: Ridding a man of Evil Spirits; the Saving of Sailors from the Tempest.

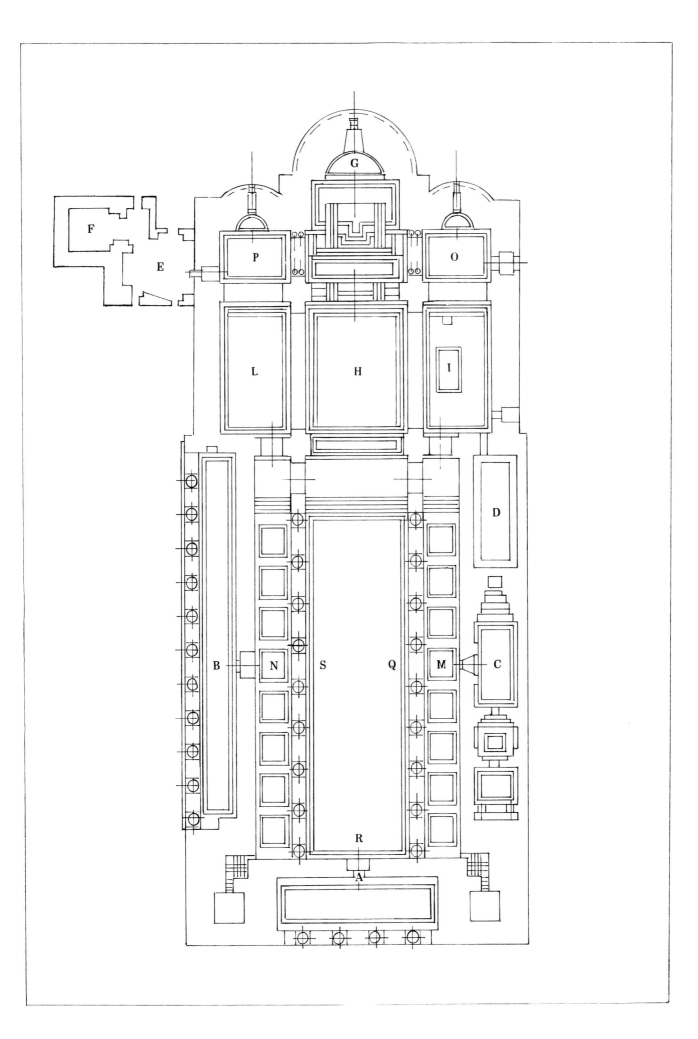